# Nature's Wonders

# THE SAHARA

## ANN HEINRICHS

**Marshall Cavendish**
Benchmark
New York

Marshall Cavendish Benchmark
99 White Plains Road
Tarrytown, NY 10591-5002
www.marshallcavendish.us

Expert Reader: Chouki El Hamel, Ph.D., Associate Professor of History, Arizona State University, Tempe

Library of Congress Cataloging-in-Publication Data
Heinrichs, Ann.
The Sahara / by Ann Heinrichs
p. cm. — (Nature's Wonders)
Summary: "Provides comprehensive information on the geography, history, wildlife, peoples,
and environmental issues of the Sahara"—Provided by publisher
Includes bibliographical references and index.
ISBN 978-0-7614-2855-8
Sahara—Juvenile literature. I. Title.
DT334.H45 2009
966—dc22
2007020326

Editor: Christine Florie
Publisher: Michelle Bisson
Art Director: Anahid Hamparian
Series Designer: Kay Petronio

Photo research by Connie Gardner

Cover photo by age fotostock/SuperStock

The photographs in this book are used by permission and through the courtesy of:
*Getty Images:* Gavin Hellier, 4; Frans Lemmens, 14, 70-71; Martin Harvey, 35; Behrouz Mehri, 83; *SuperStock:*
Christie's Images, 9; Photononstop, 10; age footstock, 13, 22, 40, 76; Jon Arnold, 86-87; Yoshi Tomii, 84; *Corbis:*
Frans Lemmens, back cover; 17, 33; Kazuyoshi Norachi, 19; Remi Benali, 28-29; Georgina Bowater, 38; Guido
Cozzi, 56; Jose Fuste Raga, 63; Denis Deighton, 67; Adam Woolfitt, 73; Wolfgang Kaehler, 79; *The Granger Collection:*
50; *The Image Works:* Topham, 24; Marcel Malherbe, 25; *Art Archive:* Bibliotheque des Arts Decoratifs Paris/Gianni
Dagli Orti, 1, 42; Musee des Arts Africains et Oceaniens/Dagli Orti, 53; *North wind Picture Archives:* 45; *Peter Arnold:*
BIOS Orgagesco-Joffe Alain J. Mallwitz, 37; Voermans Van Bree, 78; Biosphoto/Born Olivier, 90; *Photo Researchers:*
E.R. Degginger, 32; Gregory G. Dimijian, 39; *Minden Pictures:* Gertrud and Helmut Denzau/npl, 34; Cybil Ruoso,
36; *Art Resource:* Adoc-photos, 57.

Maps by Mapping Specialists Limited

Printed in China

1 3 5 6 4 2

# CONTENTS

ONE

# A Place of Mystery and Splendor

The Sahara is a place of astonishing beauty. Immense sand dunes stretch as far as the eye can see. Their graceful mounds and sharp edges sparkle in the splendor of the dazzling sun. Elsewhere, there are barren plains of black stones and stark rock formations shaped by ancient waters and winds. Gazing across this desolate landscape, one feels a boundless sense of mystery and awe. The Berber people of the Sahara call it the Garden of Allah—an empty place where God can walk in peace.

The Sahara extends all the way across North Africa. Covering about 3.5 million square miles (9 million square kilometers), it is the largest desert in the world. The Sahara is larger than the forty-eight

◄◄ The Sahara is a huge desert that covers more than 3 million square miles (9 million sq. km) of northern Africa. This is a region of the Sahara in Morocco.

## The Desert's Name

The Sahara's name comes from the Arabic word *as-sahra,* meaning "desert." Thus, it is not necessary to say "Sahara Desert." Just "Sahara" will do.

**contiguous** U.S. states and almost as large as Europe. It covers about one-fourth of the African continent. Because the Sahara is so big, people often speak of Africa in terms of two great regions: North Africa and sub-Saharan Africa.

The Sahara is one of the hottest, driest places on Earth. Few plants and animals can survive its relentless heat. But the Sahara was not always hot and dry. Thousands of years ago, its climate was warm and moist. Torrents of rain filled the rivers and lakes, and animals thrived amid lush vegetation. Then, about five thousand years ago, the climate changed and desert conditions set in.

For centuries, camel caravans crisscrossed the Sahara carrying gold and other costly trade goods. They carried ideas, too. News of the religion of Islam traveled along trade routes from North Africa deep into the continent. Great African kingdoms flourished from the wealth of the trans-Saharan trade. Tales of exotic cities such as Timbuktu lured Europeans to explore the Sahara, too.

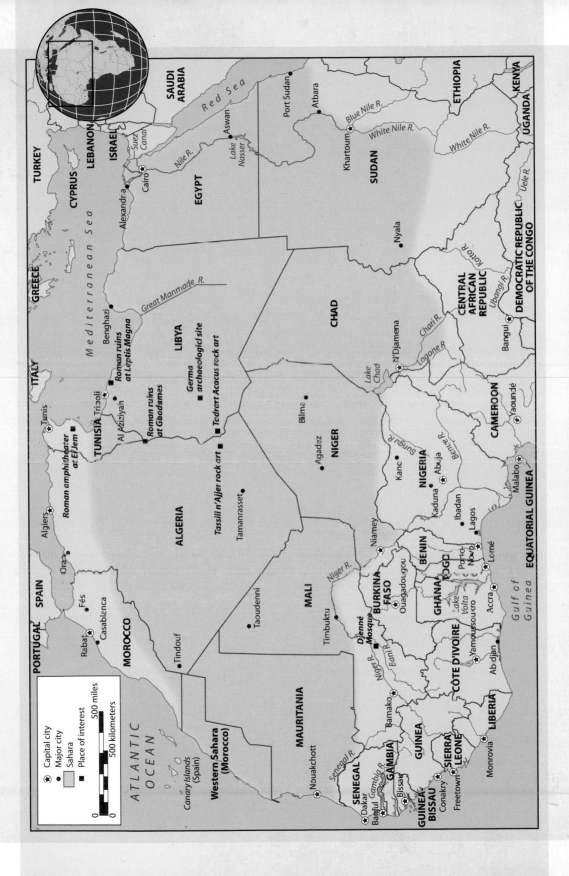

# GEOPOLITICAL MAP OF THE SAHARA

**Legend:**
- ★ Capital city
- • Major city
- Sahara
- ■ Place of interest

0 500 miles
0 500 kilometers

**Countries and regions:**
PORTUGAL, SPAIN, ITALY, GREECE, TURKEY, CYPRUS, LEBANON, ISRAEL, SAUDI ARABIA, MOROCCO, Western Sahara (Morocco), ALGERIA, TUNISIA, LIBYA, EGYPT, SUDAN, ETHIOPIA, UGANDA, KENYA, MAURITANIA, MALI, NIGER, CHAD, SENEGAL, GAMBIA, GUINEA-BISSAU, GUINEA, SIERRA LEONE, LIBERIA, CÔTE D'IVOIRE, BURKINA FASO, GHANA, TOGO, BENIN, NIGERIA, CAMEROON, EQUATORIAL GUINEA, CENTRAL AFRICAN REPUBLIC, DEMOCRATIC REPUBLIC OF THE CONGO

**Water bodies:**
ATLANTIC OCEAN, Mediterranean Sea, Red Sea, Gulf of Guinea, Canary Islands (Spain), Lake Nasser, Lake Chad, Lake Volta

**Rivers:**
Nile R., Blue Nile R., White Nile R., Great Manmade R., Niger R., Senegal R., Bani R., Benue R., Chari R., Logone R., Bangui R., Ubangi R., Uele R., Kotto R., Suez Canal

**Cities and places of interest:**
Cairo, Alexandria, Aswan, Port Sudan, Atbara, Khartoum, Nyala, Tripoli, Al Azīzīyah, Benghazi, Tunis, Algiers, Oran, Fès, Casablanca, Rabat, Tindouf, Taoudenni, Timbuktu, Tamanrasset, Agadez, Bilma, N'Djamena, Bangui, Yaoundé, Malabo, Porto-Novo, Lomé, Lagos, Ibadan, Abuja, Kaduna, Kano, Niamey, Ouagadougou, Accra, Yamoussoukro, Abidjan, Monrovia, Freetown, Conakry, Bissau, Banjul, Dakar, Nouakchott, Bamako, Djenné Mosque, Germa archaeological site, Roman ruins at Leptis Magna, Roman ruins at Ghadames, Roman amphitheater at El Jem, Tadrart Acacus rock art, Tassili n'Ajjer rock art

Today the Sahara is home to about 2.5 million people. Most live in oasis settlements, where precious water gives life to their crops. Others live as nomads. They move their herds from one location to another as the scanty rains provide pasture. Along the desert fringes, though, the population is growing. This puts pressure on the region's natural resources.

**Desertification** is one of the major environmental issues for the Sahara today. Its southern rim is gradually advancing into the bordering grasslands. Both climate change and human activities are at work here. Increased population affects the Sahara's **biodiversity** as well. Through overhunting, many once-abundant animal species

## Deserts, Hot and Cold

Strictly speaking, the icy continent of Antarctica is the largest desert on Earth. By definition, deserts are dry regions that receive little rain or snow. That is true of both Antarctica and the Sahara. Most of Antarctica's ice has been there for thousands of years. It is the world's largest cold desert, while the Sahara is the largest hot desert. Earth's many other deserts include Saudi Arabia's Arabian Desert, China's Gobi Desert, Australia's Great Victoria Desert, and Africa's Kalahari Desert.

*Richard Beavis's painting depicts a Bedouin caravan crossing the great Sahara.*

are disappearing. The need for water also threatens to deplete the Sahara's underground water supply.

Scientists, government leaders, and local organizations are working on these problems today. People around the world have joined in the effort, too. They hope the natural wonders of the Sahara will continue to enrich generations to come.

TWO

# Shaped by the Forces of Time

The world's largest desert sweeps across eleven countries in North Africa. It covers most or part of Morocco, Algeria, Tunisia, Libya, Egypt, Sudan, Chad, Niger, Mali, Mauritania, and Western Sahara.

Geographically speaking, the Sahara stretches from the Atlantic Ocean on the west to the Red Sea on the east. To the north are the Atlas Mountains and the Mediterranean Sea. (The Atlas Mountains run from southwestern Morocco, through Algeria, and into northern Tunisia.)

Where is the Sahara's southern boundary? This is not always clear. The Sahel (Arabic for "shore"), a band of semiarid grassland, runs along the desert's southern edge. However, that borderline can move.

Over the years weather satellites have observed the desert expanding to the south and retreating to the north. This shift depends partly on the amount of rainfall the border area receives. Some scientists

◄ *Formations in the Algerian region of the Sahara have been shaped by centuries of wind and water.*

also suggest that global climate change causes the Sahara to shrink and expand. Tracking the Sahara's history shows that climate change can occur on a massive scale.

## COOLER, WETTER, GREENER TIMES

Few things seem more certain than the steady march of seasons, year after year. Winter, spring, summer, and fall come and go, each with its typical weather conditions. These variations come about because of the Earth's tilt as it follows its path around the sun.

The Earth has not always kept the same position, though. Over time, it changes both the angle of its tilt and the shape of its loop around the sun. These changes have had dramatic effects on North Africa.

About ten thousand years ago, the region we know as the Sahara was lush and green. The Earth's shifts brought about heavier rains and a cooler climate. Monsoons—heavy seasonal rains—drenched the land. Rivers and lakes filled, and thick vegetation flourished. The rains and the plants actually worked together in a cycle of give-and-take. Rain produced more vegetation, and moisture from the plants evaporated, forming rain clouds.

Another great climate change took place about five thousand years ago, or around 3000 B.C.E. The Earth shifted toward the position it is in today. This time the Sahara's transformation was rather abrupt. Once the cycle of rainfall and plant growth was broken, the climate changed quickly. In the space of less than five hundred years, the once-lush Sahara became a desert, much like it is today.

*The Libyan Desert is mostly sand, though there are regions that are rocky, such as the White Desert with its chalk "mushroom" formations.*

## DESERTS WITHIN DESERTS

To understand the vast, diverse Sahara, it is helpful to look at it in sections. Some sections of the Sahara even have their own desert names.

The western section of the Sahara is sometimes called the Sahara proper. It consists mostly of sand dunes and black-gravel plains. The central Sahara is marked by several rocky mountain ranges. Among them, in northern Niger, is a stretch of desert called the Ténéré.

Most of the eastern Sahara is called the Libyan Desert. This is the harshest, most arid part of the Sahara. It stretches from eastern

Libya to the Nile River Valley of Egypt and Sudan. Egyptians often call the Libyan Desert the Western Desert, as it is west of the Nile. The portion of the Sahara between the Nile and the Red Sea is called the Arabian Desert in Egypt and the Nubian Desert in Sudan.

## ERGS: SEAS OF SAND

Picture the Sahara, and you imagine an endless sea of sand, with windswept sand dunes stretching out toward the horizon. But the Sahara is really made up of many different landscapes and landforms. Only about 15 percent of the Sahara consists of sand dunes. Most of the desert—about 70 percent—is made up of gravel-covered plains. Mountains, oases, and rocky plateaus cover the rest of the Sahara.

The Sahara's starkly beautiful stretches of sand dunes are called *ergs* (Arabic for "vein" or "belt," which has come to mean "sand sea" or "dune field"). Sand in the ergs is fine and loose, making it very difficult to cross. In some places a camel could sink up to its knees in sand.

◄ *Ergs cover about 15 percent of the Sahara. The Grand Erg Occidental covers much of Algeria.*

Sand dunes are constantly shifting, changing shape, and moving. Driven by winds, a new dune might grow overnight and disappear just as quickly. A group of dunes in the Libyan Desert moves several hundred feet every year.

Dunes in the Sahara can rise 1,000 feet (305 meters) or more, and ergs can stretch continuously across thousands of square miles. Among the Sahara's largest ergs is the Grand Erg Oriental. It is also known as the Great Eastern Erg or the Eastern Sand Sea. This expanse of sand lies mostly within Algeria, continuing into Tunisia. It covers more than 74,000 square miles (192,000 sq. km). That is larger than the state of Washington.

Another massive sea of sand is Algeria's Grand Erg Occidental (Great Western Erg or Western Sand Sea). Others include Egypt's

## Beware of Fech Fech!

One hazard for Sahara travelers is *fech fech* (pronounced *fesh fesh*). This fine-grained dust is soft and powdery, like flour. Although it looks like sand, it is composed of worn-down clay and rock. Fech fech covers large areas of Egypt's Qattara Depression. However, it occurs in many places throughout the Sahara.

There is no way to tell where the fech fech is. A vehicle can suddenly sink deep into fech fech as if it were quicksand. The fine dust is almost impossible to dig, so the vehicle is trapped—for hours, for days, or forever.

# Dune Shapes

Sand dunes occur in many diverse shapes. Their form depends on the direction and force of winds. The most common dune shape is crescentic, or crescent shaped. These dunes are also called barchan dunes. They look like gently rounded hills with a deep curve gouged out of one side. Two long arms, called horns, stretch out on each side. Crescent-shaped dunes are formed by heavy winds blowing in one direction. They are common in Algeria's Great Western Erg.

Star dunes are cone shaped, with arms extending down from the top in several directions. They are created in areas where the winds blow in many directions. Star dunes are prominent in the Great Eastern Erg.

Linear dunes occur in long, narrow lines that may stretch for miles. A linear dune is sometimes called a *seif*, the Arabic word for "sword," because of its sharp ridge. Often appearing in wide-open basins, linear dunes run in the direction of prevailing winds. They are commonly seen in the western Sahara. Geologists have also defined many other dune shapes formed by complex wind patterns.

Great Sand Sea, Libya's Idehan Murzuq, Niger's Great Bilma Erg, and Algeria's Erg Chech.

Not all of the Sahara's sands are piled into dunes. There are also firm, flat plains of sand, such as the Selima Sand Sheet. It covers tens of thousands of square miles in northwestern Sudan and southwestern Egypt.

## REGS: TERROR AND THIRST

A bleak and barren plain stretches across southwestern Algeria, reaching over the border into Mali. Once a traveler enters it, there will be no water, no vegetation, no landmarks, and no letup from the sun's relentless rays. This forbidding landscape is the Tanezrouft. Local people call it the Land of Terror or the Land of Thirst.

The Tanezrouft, an ancient lakebed, is one of the most desolate parts of the Sahara. If caravanners dared to cross it, they risked their lives. An 1809 expedition in the Tanezrouft came across 2,000 corpses of caravanners and 1,800 corpses of camels. Another grim discovery came in the 1980s. Explorers found the remains of a group of Algerian soldiers in the Tanezrouft who had become lost in the 1950s. All had died of thirst and exposure to the intense heat.

The Tanezrouft is one of the Sahara's *regs*. (The word *reg* is common in the western Sahara, while *serir* is usually used in the eastern Sahara. *Reg* is Arabic for "stone," and *serir* is Arabic for "bed.") Sometimes called stone deserts, regs make up most of the Saharan landscape. They are rough plains covered with coarse gravel and rocks. Often

*Mount Ilamen is one of the highest peaks in the Algerian mountains.*

the gravel is black, but some regs may have red or white gravel. A thin layer of drifting sand may overlay the reg's rocky surface.

The Sahara's most famous reg is the Tanezrouft, but the largest is the Libyan Desert's Libyan Reg. Its size is hard to establish, but it has been estimated to cover as much as 340,000 square miles (880,600 sq. km). Another large reg stretches across Niger's Ténéré region.

## MOUNTAINS AND PLATEAUS

In the central Sahara, steep mountain masses rise sharply above the surrounding plains. These clusters of mountains are often called

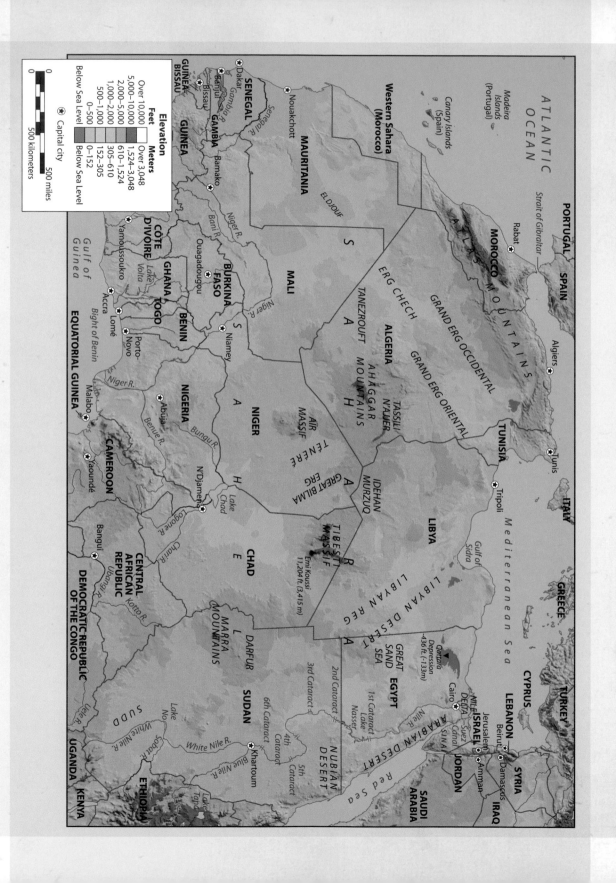

PHYSICAL MAP OF THE SAHARA

**massifs**. Their crevices and deep ravines once made good hideouts for bandits who preyed on passing caravans.

The Sahara's largest and highest mountain range is the Tibesti Massif of northern Chad. The Tibesti peaks are volcanoes that are dormant, or no longer active. Emi Koussi, the highest mountain in this range, is the Sahara's highest peak.

The Ahaggar Mountains of southern Algeria are a chain of jagged peaks separated by high, rocky desert terrain. The main city in the Ahaggar region is the oasis town of Tamanrasset. The granite mountains of the Aïr Massif rise in north-central Niger. Deep valleys nestle among its peaks, and people can graze camels and goats there. Agadez, at the southern foot of the range, is the capital of the Aïr region.

Scattered throughout the Sahara are bare, rocky plateaus called *hamadas* (Arabic for "dead" or "lifeless"). On many of these plateaus, wind and water have carved the rock into strange shapes. Some plateaus are small, while others cover thousands of square miles. It used to take a week or more for camel caravans to cross western Libya's Hamada al Hamra.

The Tassili n'Ajjer of southeastern Algeria is an immense plateau region. (*Tassili* means "plateau" in the language of the local Tuareg people.) It is often considered a mountain range. Ancient rivers have carved about three hundred stone arches out of the sandstone. The Tassili n'Ajjer is also famous for its ancient rock paintings. Much of this region is protected as a national park.

# WATER, WATER, EVERYWHERE

Gaze across the Sahara or take a deep breath of its air. The sheer dryness is overwhelming. Who would imagine that billions of gallons of water lie underground? In fact the Sahara covers some of the world's most abundant aquifers, or underground water systems. They are remnants of earlier times, when rainwater was plentiful. The water soaked into the ground, where it collected in layers of rock.

*More than three hundred stone arches in Algeria's Tassili n' Ajjer were carved by prehistoric rivers.*

Some of the world's largest aquifers lie beneath the Sahara. One is the North-Western Sahara Aquifer System, underlying Algeria, Libya, and Tunisia. Another is the Nubian Sandstone Aquifer System, beneath Chad, Egypt, Libya, and Sudan. It is believed to be the largest aquifer in the world.

Not all of the Sahara's underground water is fresh and drinkable. In some places, minerals in the soil make the water salty or give it an awful taste. Some maps of the Sahara show the location of springs, wells, and waterholes. They also include a description of the water, telling whether it is good to drink, somewhat drinkable, or salty. This is valuable information for desert travelers.

## A Renewable Resource?

When people dig a well in the Sahara, they are tapping into an aquifer. Sometimes they find water fairly close to the surface. But often people must dig or drill hundreds of feet to reach water. They may have to go through many layers of soil, sand, gravel, or porous rock. The level at which the ground is fully saturated with water is called the water table. The more water people draw from aquifers, the more the water table drops. Technically speaking, water from the aquifers is a renewable resource. That means it can be replaced naturally.

In the case of aquifers, they can recharge, or refill with new rainwater. However, many aquifers contain water reserves called fossil water. It was deposited thousands or even millions of years ago. Of course these aquifers can refill—given enough time. In some regions of the Sahara, however, people are drawing water from aquifers at many times the estimated recharge rate.

## Islands in the Sea of Sand

Here and there across the sandy landscape, a clump of palm trees suddenly appears. They are the welcome signs of an oasis. Oases are spots where underground water rises to the surface, giving life to lush vegetation. They are sometimes called islands in a sea of sand.

How does the water in an oasis come to the surface? Often it gushes up naturally, creating something called an artesian spring. Sometimes people dig wells, tunneling down until they reach water.

*Some underground waters in the Sahara rise to the surface, creating fertile oases.*

They may use a pump to bring the water to the surface. An oasis may also get its water from a river, a lake, or an irrigation system built out from a water source.

## RIVERS, LAKES, WADIS, AND CHOTTS

The major river in the Sahara is the Nile River of Egypt and Sudan. Thanks to this strip of moisture, the Nile River Valley flourishes with crops, fruit trees, palm trees, and other lush vegetation. The Niger River winds along the southwest edge of the Sahara. These two waterways are the Sahara's only permanent rivers.

Wadis are seasonal streams that are dry most of the time. Sudden, violent downpours of rain can flood the wadis with rushing water. Wadis can also fill with water running down from mountains. Eventually the water evaporates or soaks into the ground, leaving dry riverbeds.

Lake Chad is the Sahara's largest lake. It lies at the point where the borders of Niger, Chad, and Nigeria meet. Lake Chad is a shallow lake that swells during rainy seasons and shrinks during dry periods. Thousands of years ago it was a massive lake, covering as much as 154,500 square miles (400,000 sq. km). As the Sahara's climate changed, most of the lake dried up.

Libya has several sparkling, palm-fringed lakes. They are nestled among the giant sand dunes of the Ubari Sand Sea. Elsewhere in the Sahara, seasonal rains create small, short-lived ponds and pools.

Chotts are dried-up salt lakes. They are also known as salt pans. During dry seasons they are wide, flat depressions covered with a crusty layer of salt crystals. When it rains, chotts fill with water.

*Feluccas sail on the Sahara's largest river, the Nile*

The water is salty and undrinkable, though. Tunisia's Chott el-Djerid covers hundreds of square miles.

## HEAT

The Sahara is one of the hottest places on Earth. During the day, temperatures can be unbearable. In the summer (roughly April through September), daytime temperatures often average 90 degrees to 110 degrees Fahrenheit (32° to 43 °Celsius), but many parts of the desert get even hotter. Al Aziziyah, Libya, recorded the world's highest official temperature of all time in 1922. The temperature soared to 136 °F (58 °C).

Temperatures are cooler in the winter (roughly October through March), averaging about 50 °F to 60 °F (10 °C to 16 °C) in the daytime. But in all seasons the desert temperature plunges at night. That is because the sandy soil cannot hold heat.

## HOW DRY IS DRY?

The Sahara may be hot, but dryness is what makes it a desert. Not all deserts are hot, but lack of moisture is a desert's number-one feature. How dry is a desert? By one definition, a desert is land that gets an average of less than 10 inches (25 centimeters) of precipitation a year. The Sahara certainly passes that test with an average of about 3 inches (76 millimeters) of precipitation a year.

The Sahara's northern and southern edges get the most rainfall. The high mountaintops of the central Sahara even get snow in the winter. But some regions of the desert get little rain, or none at all. Some spots get heavy rain for a week, followed by years of no rain. In the Selima Sand Sheet of Egypt and Sudan, it rains two or three times in a *century!*

The terms *winter* and *summer* do not exactly make sense for the Sahara. Instead, residents tend to think in terms of wet and dry seasons. The Sahara's rain schedule is a bit complicated, though, and can vary from year to year and from place to place.

In the northern Sahara, rain usually falls in December through March, followed by a very dry season. Heavy thunderstorms come in August, sometimes causing flash floods. In the southern Sahara, November through March are hot and dry. Then begins the rainy season, with the heaviest downpours in July and August.

## Saharan Dust: A Worldwide Traveler

The Sahara is the major source of aeolian, or windborne, dust in the world. Dust stirred up in a Sahara windstorm travels through the atmosphere to Europe, the United States, and South America. British scientists have measured 10 million tons of Saharan dust deposited in Great Britain from a single storm! In the United States, Saharan dust sometimes reaches Florida, causing a hazy cloud that blocks the sun. Windborne dust from the Sahara also provides nutrients to the canopy, or leafy upper layer, of Brazil's Amazon rain forest.

# They Call the Winds by Name

Strong winds whip through the Sahara for days on end. They can whisk tons of sand and dust through the air, making it impossible for travelers to see. Once the winds die down, the landscape has changed completely.

People of the Sahara have given names to their windstorms. The *harmattan* (possibly from the Arabic word for "evil thing") gusts across the southern Sahara in the winter. It picks up tons of dust and carries it hundreds of miles out over the Atlantic Ocean. Egypt's late-winter *khamsin* (Arabic for "fifty") blows on and off for about fifty days.

The *haboob* of the Sudan comes in the summer and lasts only a few

hours. Its name comes from the Arabic term for "strong wind." It drives huge clouds of sand and dust and often comes with thunderstorms. In Algeria and Tunisia summertime brings the *sirocco*, locally called the *chehili*, *qibli*, or *ghibli* (its various names derive from the Arabic *sharqi*, meaning "easterly," and *qibli*, meaning "coming from the direction of Mecca"). This hot, dry wind blows northward across the Sahara. It makes temperatures soar and deposits dust everywhere.

The deadly *simoom* (Arabic for "poison wind") strikes in the summer. In less than an hour the simoom's scorching heat and swirling dust clouds can kill both animals and people. They suffocate or die of heat stroke. Local people take cover when the simoom comes. They know they must respect its power in order to survive.

*A shepherd guides his goats and sheep home as a sandstorm approaches his village in Mali.*

# THREE

# Wildlife of the Sahara

For plants and animals, surviving in the Sahara is a challenge. Every day they face three life-threatening conditions: lack of water, lack of food, and intense heat. It would seem that life is impossible in such a harsh environment. Yet, somehow, the Sahara's creatures do manage to find nourishment and reproduce. They have developed amazing strategies for adapting to hot, dry conditions.

## ANIMALS OF EARLIER TIMES

Before looking at today's wildlife, imagine how different the Sahara's animals were in earlier times. Ten thousand years ago water and food were abundant. With lush grazing lands and rich hunting grounds, large animals had plenty to eat. Hippopotamuses swam in the lakes and wallowed on the muddy banks. Long-legged giraffes munched on succulent tree leaves, while buffaloes, elephants, rhinoceroses, and warthogs ranged across the savanna.

◀ *Though the Sahara is hot and dry, wild animals such as this Dorcas gazelle find a way to survive there.*

We know about these animals from the Sahara's rock art. Thousands of years ago, people carved and painted scenes from their environment. They depicted not only animals, but also everyday activities such as hunting, herding, and farming. Much of this art appears in protected places—inside caves, on cliff faces, or under overhanging rocks.

## LIVING SMALL, KEEPING COOL

Today the desert environment cannot support a host of large animals. Most of the Sahara's animals are small. Saharan mammals include dozens of species of rodents, such as jerboas, gerbils, and mice. Jerboas, with their long hind legs, are speedy runners and good jumpers. The spiny mouse has stiff hair and big eyes and ears. It darts in and out of rocky spaces looking for seeds and insects.

*The jerboa can grow as long as 16 inches, but 10 of these inches are its tail!*

To keep cool, most of these animals burrow into the sand or nestle in rock crevices. They spend their days napping or resting to escape the blistering heat. At night they come out to hunt or forage for food. One exception is a chunky little rodent called the gundi. It often sits on a rock out in the sun. Gundis use the comblike bristles on their feet to groom their fur. When a predator comes along, the gundi rolls on its side and plays dead.

## DESERT CARNIVORES

Foxes, weasels, jackals, hyenas, and cheetahs are some of the Sahara's carnivores, or meat eaters. The smaller carnivores prey on rodents, lizards, insects, and other small creatures. Larger species go after antelopes, gazelles, and domestic animals such as sheep and goats.

*Fennecs live in the Sahara and avoid the daytime heat by hunting during the night.*

The Sahara's fennec is a long-eared little fox. It is the smallest of all fox species, weighing only about 2 pounds (1 kilogram). Fennecs are about 15 inches (38 cm) long, but their ears can grow 6 inches (15 cm) or more. With these big ears they can hear burrowing insects and other small creatures. Fennecs' long, thick, sand-colored fur blends in well with their desert environment. The soles of their feet are hairy, too, to protect them from the hot sand. Other Sahara foxes include the pale fox and the sand fox.

Jackals and hyenas are large predators that are seen roaming around populated areas. People kill them, often by poisoning, because they prey on flocks of sheep and goats. Herding is a vital way of life here, and families depend on their livestock to stay alive.

## CATS, BIG AND SMALL

Lions roamed the Sahara in earlier times, when water and vegetation were plentiful there. By now, however, these big carnivores mostly live south of the Sahara. The only "big cat" in the Sahara today is the cheetah.

Cheetahs are among the rarest large animals in the Sahara. In fact the Sahara is one of the last places in the world where cheetahs live in the wild. Little by little, humans have been moving in on the cheetahs' natural habitat. Now these sleek, spotted cats roam the mountainous regions of Algeria, Mali, Niger, and Chad. Sometimes they range out onto the plains in search of prey such as gazelles.

Another Sahara feline is the sand cat. It is one of the smallest of all cat species. Sand cats have small, round bodies, short legs, and big ears. Their sand-colored fur blends perfectly into their

*The sand cat has adapted to its environment with a coat that keeps it warm during the cold desert nights and with feet that are covered with long hair to protect it from the hot daytime sands.*

## An Unusual Cat

Cheetahs are the fastest known land animals. They can run faster than 65 miles (105 km) an hour. Their large nostrils help them take in more oxygen when they run. Cheetahs differ from other big cats such as lions in many ways. While other big cats hunt by sneaking up on their prey, cheetahs hunt by chasing animals at high speed. Cheetahs hunt by day, while others tend to hunt at night. Also, unlike other big cats, cheetahs can purr while inhaling and they cannot roar.

surroundings. A heavy layer of hair covers their foot pads so they can safely walk across the scorching sand. However, they usually spend their days under rock ledges or in burrows they dig in the sand.

Sand cats come out to hunt at night, when temperatures are cooler. With their big ears, they can hear very small movements and high-pitched squeaks. They hunt jerboas and other rodents, as well as lizards, birds, insects, and even snakes. Most of their water comes from the food they eat.

*A desert addax rests during the heat of the day.*

## ANTELOPES, GAZELLES, AND MOUNTAIN SHEEP

Several species of antelope and gazelle live in the Sahara. These graceful, slender-legged animals have long horns and they usually travel in groups. Their bodies have adapted to the desert heat so they do not have to sweat very much. Other animals sweat to cool off. But for desert dwellers, sweating would deplete vital bodily fluids.

The desert addax, a type of antelope, has wide, flat hooves for walking in the sand without sinking in. Addaxes dig hollows in the sand to create shelters. These amazing animals can go for months or even years without drinking water. They get their moisture from the plant leaves they nibble.

Addaxes often cross miles of desert wasteland to reach vegetation. They have a way of sensing that rain is coming from up to 125 miles (200 km) away. At once, they take off in the direction of the rain showers, where they know they will find fresh, green pastures.

Dama gazelles are the largest of all gazelle species. Like addaxes, they get most of their moisture from plants. They graze on desert shrubs, grasses, and the leaves of the acacia tree. During dry seasons, they move toward the Sahel. When the rainy season comes they move back into the desert. Dama gazelles were once the most numerous of all the Sahara's gazelles. Now only small herds remain in Chad, Niger, and Mali.

Tiny dorcas gazelles can live their whole lives without drinking water. They are speedy runners, moving across the landscape in bouncing leaps. These gazelles sometimes stand on their hind legs to eat the succulent leaves of acacia trees.

Barbary sheep, with their curved horns, live in the arid mountains of the Sahara. Nimble and sure-footed on the rocky mountainsides, they can jump more than 6 feet (2 m) from a standing position. Barbary sheep graze on whatever they can find among the jagged rocks—grasses, bushes, and tree leaves. All the moisture they need comes from plants. However, if they do find water, they will drink it and even wallow in it.

*Native to North Africa, Barbary sheep can be found in the mountain regions of the Sahara.*

# Ships of the Desert

Camels are well built for desert survival. Their wide-bottomed hooves are good for walking in sand. Because they seem to glide so smoothly across the sea of sand, they are often called ships of the desert.

Camels have thick eyelashes to keep sand out of their eyes. Each eye has two eyelids. When sand and dust are blowing around, camels close their transparent inner lid. It protects the eye, but the camel can still see.

Camels can live without water and food much longer than other animals. Their humps are full of energy-rich fatty tissue that can be converted into nutrients. A camel can go without water for about two weeks. It can survive as long as a month without eating food.

## BIRDS AND OTHER CREATURES

Desert eagle owls soar through the skies above the desert. Their wingspans can reach 4 feet (1.2 m). Desert vultures cruise the arid landscape for dead animals to eat. On the ground, large Houbara bustards search for rodents and lizards.

The Sahara's lakes and pools are home to shrimp and other tiny shellfish. Toads and frogs live there, too. Little Mauritanian toads bury themselves in the mud of temporary pools that eventually dry

*A horned viper conceals itself in the sand of the Sahara, ready to strike its prey with its deadly venom.*

up. They stay buried until it rains again. Land snails also inhabit the Sahara. They survive by becoming dormant, or inactive, during dry spells. They may stay this way for years until it rains again.

Horned vipers, sand vipers, and cobras slink among the Sahara's rocks and dunes. Horned vipers are venomous and stealthy. They burrow into the sand so they cannot be seen. When they hear something—or someone—approaching, they spring out and strike. Other Sahara reptiles include chameleons and spiny-tailed lizards. Ants, lice, centipedes, millipedes, spiders, and scorpions scuttle across the desert floor. Of the Sahara's thirty scorpion species, four can be deadly to humans.

## PLANT LIFE

Plant life in the Sahara is sparse. Most trees, shrubs, and grasses grow in the oases. Many plants also grow on the Sahara's northern and southern fringes, where there is more rainfall. The highlands and the wadis have enough moisture to support plant life, too. On the dry plains and plateaus are plants that have adapted to heat and drought.

Most Saharan plants are ephemeral plants or xerophytes. Ephemeral plants have a short life span. They spring to life after a rainfall. Within a few weeks, they mature, produce seeds, and die. Their seeds lie in wait for the next rainfall, which may be months—or years—away. When it rains, ephemeral grasses sprout up to make pastures called *acheb* (Arabic for "grass").

Xerophytes are plants that have ways of conserving water. They take in water when it rains and store it to use later. One example is euphorbia, which grows in much of the Sahara. This cactuslike plant stores water in its stem and oozes a milky sap.

## TREES

A few scattered acacias might be the only plants in sight across miles of sandy plains. Acacias are the hardiest trees in the Sahara. They can grow in places that get only 1 inch (2.5 cm) of rain a year. Acacias have a root system that enables them to survive in the desert. The

*Acacias thrive in the desert where they can survive on at least 1 inch (2.5 cm) of rain per year.*

# The Tree of Ténéré

For three hundred years a lone acacia stood upon the sandy expanse of Niger's Ténéré Desert. It was the last survivor of an ancient forest that once covered the region. By the twentieth century, no other trees were to be found for 250 miles (400 km).

For caravans on the way to the Bilma salt fields, the tree was a cherished landmark. Known as *L'Arbre du Ténéré* (Tree of Ténéré), it was even shown on the Michelin map of northwest Africa. Sadly, in 1973, a truck driver ran into the tree and knocked it down. Now a metal sculpture of a tree stands in its place.

long, central taproot grows straight down to reach water. One famous acacia—the Tree of Ténéré—had a taproot 130 feet (40 m) long.

Date palms are the most common trees in the oases. They can grow 75 feet (23 m) tall and live for 150 years. The sugary dates they yield are a favorite dessert. The much shorter doum palm grows in the highlands. It bears a fruit that looks like an apple. Olive and cypress trees grow in the highlands, too.

Tamarisks grow as shrubs or trees and produce clusters of pink flowers. Both people and animals like to bask in the shade of their leafy branches. Tamarisks can withstand drought and salty soil. Like acacias, they grow deep roots. Like humans, they survive on the life-sustaining waters that flow underground.

# FOUR

# Exploring the Great Desert

Over the centuries many empires gained control of the North African coast. But the invaders rarely ventured into the desert. Their mission was not exploration. It was to establish colonies and trade centers along the Mediterranean Sea. Visitors to these cities brought back news of the great desert. In time, explorers would trek across the Sahara in hopes of solving its mysteries. For some, that quest brought rich rewards. For others, it was deadly.

## ANCIENT TALES

Some of the earliest written reports of the Sahara come from the Greek historian Herodotus, who lived in the 400s B.C.E. Often called the Father of History, Herodotus gathered information from his own travels and the tales of other adventurers. This is how he described the Libyan Desert: "Above the coast-line and the country inhabited by the maritime peoples, Libya is full of wild beasts; while beyond the wild beast region there is a tract which is wholly sand, very scant of water, and utterly and entirely a desert."

◄ *Sahara crossings were made by people in trade caravans, as well as by explorers hoping to uncover its mysteries.*

In Herodotus's time the Phoenicians had colonies in North Africa. These seafaring traders originated in today's Lebanon and Syria. The greatest Phoenician trade center in Africa was Carthage. It flourished near present-day Tunis, Tunisia. The Carthaginians made no journeys into the Sahara, but local Berber tribespeople did. Berber merchants brought trade goods from Africa's interior through the Sahara to Carthage. Beyond their well-traveled trade routes, however, even the Berbers found the Sahara an unknown land.

Many ancient writers told of the Sahara and its people. Yet none of these writers had been there or even heard firsthand accounts. Some writers simply repeated what earlier accounts had said. For centuries fabulous tales circulated about tiny people, kingdoms of gold, and other Sahara legends. Only in the 1300s C.E. did accurate information about the Sahara come to light. Arab scholars and travelers brought the news.

## ARAB AND MUSLIM EXPLORATIONS

In Arabia, to the east of Africa, the religion of Islam arose in the 600s C.E. Muslims, the followers of Islam, spread their faith over a vast expanse of lands. They reached from today's Afghanistan to the east, across North Africa, and into Spain to the west. Muslim Arab scholars and scientists built great centers of learning. Traveling by camel, Arab merchants trekked deep into the Sahara in trade caravans.

*An Arab caravan crosses the Sahara, bringing with it a wealth of tradition and culture.*

One Sahara crossing took place on such a lavish scale that it still seems astounding today. The traveler was Mansa Musa, king of the West African empire of Mali. A devout Muslim, Musa used his great wealth from the trans-Sahara trade to build mosques and universities. In 1324 he set off on a hajj, or pilgrimage, to the Muslim holy city of Mecca in Arabia. To get there he crossed the Sahara in a magnificent caravan, with thousands of richly dressed officials, soldiers, servants, and slaves, as well as eighty camels laden with gold. They trekked through the desert sands to Cairo, where Musa gave away mass quantities of gold. Then he continued on to Mecca and returned across the Sahara again. Musa's journey, and his fabulous wealth and generosity, made Mali famous throughout the Arab world and in Europe as well.

Mansa Musa was still traveling when Ibn Battuta began his own journey. Born in present-day Morocco, he would become the greatest traveler of his time. Ibn Battuta had already covered much of the known world by 1352, when he joined a trade caravan bound for the empire of Mali. There he met the emperor Mansa Suleyman, Mansa Musa's brother. Then he traveled to Timbuktu, where he was impressed with the city's many schools. The old traveler got back home to Morroco early in 1354 and dictated an account of his many journeys.

Leo Africanus was another great Sahara traveler. Africanus was born in 1485 as Hassan Ibn Muhammad Al Wazzan. Born in Muslim-occupied Spain, he grew up in Fez, Morocco. Following the camel

# The Great Traveler

Ibn Battuta (1304–1368?) is called the greatest traveler of medieval times. He covered more territory and visited more countries than anyone else in the Middle Ages. Born in Tangier, in present-day Morocco, Ibn Battuta was a devout, well-educated Muslim. He decided to visit the full extent of Muslim lands, promising himself "never to travel any road a second time." Ibn Battuta spent almost thirty years of his life traveling. In that time, he covered an amazing 75,000 miles (120,700 km). On a modern map the lands he visited fall within more than forty countries.

caravan routes, Africanus traveled deep into the Sahara. He visited Timbuktu twice and visited the sultans of other great West African kingdoms in present-day Mali and Nigeria. He described Timbuktu as a place of great wealth.

> The rich king of Tombuto [Timbuktu] hath many plates and sceptres of gold, some whereof weigh 1,300 pounds. . . . He hath always 3,000 horsemen . . . [and] a great store of doctors, judges, priests, and other learned men that are bountifully maintained at the king's expense.

## Europeans Begin the Quest

Europeans had read about the Sahara for centuries. But they did not begin their own explorations until the late 1700s. Saharan lands had long been under the control of Muslim kingdoms and African tribespeople. But adventurous Europeans were determined to penetrate the mysteries of these far-off lands.

Several early explorations were sponsored by a British society called the African Association. Its full name was the Association for Promoting the Discovery of the Interior Parts of Africa. Its members were mostly "armchair explorers"—upper-class gentlemen who were curious about "exotic" Africa. Two burning questions occupied their minds: what was the course of the great Niger River, and where was the fabled city of Timbuktu?

In 1790 the association sent Irish explorer Daniel Houghton to find Timbuktu. Starting on the West African coast, Houghton traveled inland toward the Niger River, which led to Timbuktu. But Houghton simply disappeared. Later it was found that his guides had robbed and deserted him in the Sahara. According to one account, "He wandered about the desert, alone, and famishing, till, utterly exhausted, he lay down under a tree and expired."

## Mungo Park

Houghton's fate put a damper on future explorations. Yet, nothing could daunt the fearless Scotsman Mungo Park (1771–1806). In 1795 the African Association sent him to explore the Niger River.

## From Here to Timbuktu

Timbuktu—or Tombouctou in French—was a great center for the trans-Sahara trade. Tuareg nomads founded the city in the eleventh century. In time, Berber, Arabic, and Jewish traders met there to buy and sell gold, ivory, and salt. Timbuktu's kings were known to be fabulously wealthy. The city was also an Islamic intellectual center. Its three great mosques—Djingareyber, Sankore, and Sidi Yahya—are among the oldest in Africa. Their libraries housed hundreds of manuscripts on religion, history, geography, astronomy, medicine, and many other subjects. For Europeans, Timbuktu seemed a faraway legend. The phrase "from here to Timbuktu" became a symbol for travel to distant, exotic lands.

A year later—after being robbed, beaten, and imprisoned—Park reached Ségou, in present-day Mali. There, at last, he gazed upon the Niger River. He wrote with joy about finding "the long-sought-for majestic Niger, glittering in the morning sun. . . . I hastened to the brink, and having drunk of the water, I lifted up my fervent thanks in prayer."

Park was the first European to reach the Niger River. But no one knew it at the time. Hearing no reports from Park, the African Association gave him up for dead. But in 1797 Britain's armchair explorers got a big surprise: sick and bedraggled, Mungo Park showed up in England again. He was hailed as a hero, and his book *Travels in the Interior Districts of Africa* became an instant best seller.

*Scottsman Mungo Park, was twice hired by the African Association to explore the Niger River.*

In 1805 the African Association rewarded him with another expedition. He was to explore the Niger River to its mouth. This time he was equipped with more than forty men.

Park began his expedition in high spirits, writing to a friend that "[in] six weeks, I expect to drink all your healths in the Niger." But things went terribly wrong. His party set out during West Africa's rainy season, which made travel treacherously difficult. Lions and crocodiles were a constant danger, too. One by one, Park's men drowned, got lost, or died of dysentery and other diseases. By the time he reached the Niger at Bamako (Mali), only eleven men were still alive. According to one account, they were "all sick, and some in a state of mental derangement."

Park rested for a couple of months and had his men build a sort of canoe to continue down the Niger. Meanwhile, he wrote letters back to England with his usual reckless optimism. He would reach the mouth of the Niger, he boasted, and would probably be back in England before the letter arrived!

Park set sail in November 1805 with only six men alive and well enough to travel. In spite of frequent attacks by local people, they covered an amazing 1,000 miles (1,600 km) of the Niger's course. But the explorations of Mungo Park would soon come to an end.

At Bussa Rapids, in today's Nigeria, Park's party was attacked. Five men, including Park, drowned while trying to escape. Only their native guide survived to tell the tale.

## THE DANGEROUS ROAD TO TIMBUKTU

The Niger River was important for trade. It could transport goods from south of the Sahara to trade centers such as Timbuktu. But for European explorers, the city of Timbuktu itself remained an unclaimed prize. As the centuries passed, this city of unimaginable riches became ever more alluring. Did this fabled City of Gold even exist?

Great Britain's African Association was determined to find out. In 1797 they hired a young German explorer named Friedrich Hornemann (1772–1801). Starting from Cairo, Egypt, he was to cross the Sahara to Timbuktu.

In Cairo, Hornemann disguised himself as a Muslim and joined a trade caravan to Murzuk. This oasis town, called the Paris of the Sahara, lay in the Fezzan region of southwestern Libya. It was the jumping-off point for caravans to Lake Chad and the Niger River. Hornemann finally left Murzuk by caravan in 1800. He was never heard from again. Later he was spotted in northern Nigeria, where he is believed to have died.

Soon the British government began sponsoring African explorations. With colonies all over the world, Great Britain hoped to add African lands to its empire. A bustling trade center such as Timbuktu would be a great conquest.

In 1825 a young Scotsman named Major Alexander Gordon Laing (1793–1826) was sent to Timbuktu. To get there, he would begin in Tripoli (Libya) and cross the Sahara. This 2,000-mile (3,220-km) trip was the long way to Timbuktu. But the shorter route, traveling inland from Morocco or the west coast, was considered too dangerous to try.

Laing figured his trip would take a few weeks, but he misjudged the rigors of Sahara travel. It took him 399 days—about fifty weeks longer than he had thought. Along the way he was racked by loneliness and fever. He baked in the blistering sun by day and shivered on the desert floor by night. Betrayed by his guide, he was attacked by bandits, who left him with two dozen wounds.

With festering cuts and a case of yellow fever, Laing entered the famous City of Gold in August 1826. He was the first European to reach Timbuktu. The city had declined over time, though, and it now seemed a shabby little town. Timbuktu's kings once lived in grand palaces, but now, Timbuktu's governor occupied a small, mud house. Laing stayed for a month and was murdered on his way out of town.

## LIVING TO TELL THE TALE

France had its eye on Timbuktu as well. In 1824 France's Société de Géographie (Geographical Society) announced a prize to entice explorers. It would pay ten thousand francs to the first European to reach Timbuktu—and live to tell about it. This offer appealed to the French explorer René Caillié (1799–1838).

Caillié had grown up reading the adventure novel *Robinson Crusoe.* At age sixteen, eager to have his own adventures, he sailed to Senegal on the West African coast. When he heard about the Timbuktu prize, he was sure he could win it.

For months Caillié lived among African Muslims. He learned Arabic, converted to Islam, and studied Muslim customs. In 1827 he set off on his journey from the West African coast. At the time he had no idea that Laing had already reached Timbuktu.

*Explorer René Caillié dressed as an Arab during his trips to help him blend in with the local people.*

Dressed as an Arab, Caillié claimed to be returning to his home in Egypt. Unlike earlier explorers, he mixed easily with local people. In April 1828 he reached Timbuktu, where he spent two weeks. Then he joined a caravan heading to Morocco and crossed the Sahara from south to north. On returning to France, he received the ten thousand-franc prize and was awarded the distinguished Legion of Honor.

Caillié's adventures inspired many other explorers. One was the Englishman John Davidson. In 1836 he left Morocco for Timbuktu, but he was murdered before he got there. Heinrich Barth had better luck. This German explorer knew Arabic and had traveled widely in the Middle East. From 1850 to 1855 he undertook a long expedition for the British government. After his two fellow explorers died, Barth carried on alone, traveling from Tripoli to Lake Chad to Timbuktu and back again. He, too, lived to tell the tale.

## THE SCRAMBLE FOR AFRICA

Many other explorers crisscrossed the Sahara in the 1800s. They mapped its landscape and studied its people and cultures. Eventually, though, sheer exploration gave way to economic, military, and political aims. European powers began competing with each other to claim African territories. This came to be called the Scramble for Africa. By the late 1800s European powers had carved up most of the continent. Great Britain, France, Germany, Portugal, Italy, Spain, and Belgium each ruled chunks of Africa.

In the Sahara region, France became the major power. France eventually controlled Morocco, Senegal, Mauritania, Mali, Algeria, Niger, Chad, and Tunisia. Great Britain occupied Egypt and Sudan. Italy gained control of Libya, while Spain ruled what is now Western Sahara.

Under European colonial rule, more detailed studies were made of the Sahara. By the early 1900s most of the desert had been explored and mapped. New maps of the Sahara showed its oases, mountains, sandy wastelands, and traditional travel routes.

With newly invented motor vehicles, people could travel the

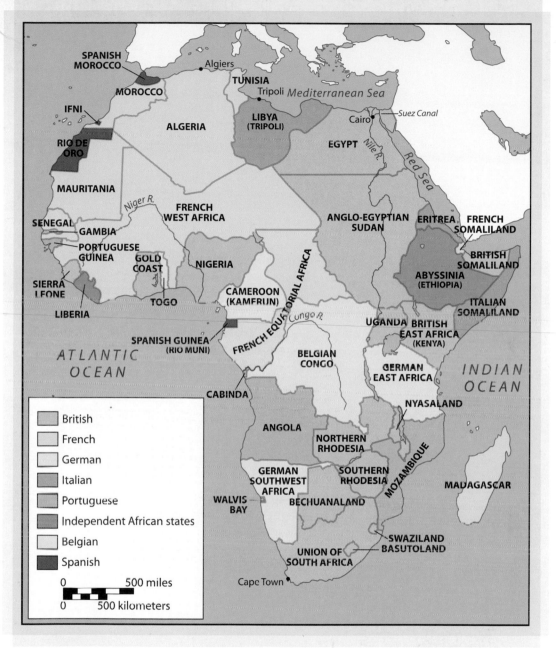

Sahara by automobile. From 1922 to 1923 Georges-Marie Haardt and Louis Audouin-Dubreuil became the first to cross the Sahara by motor car. Their twenty-one-day, north–south route went from

Touggourt, Algeria, to Timbuktu. Their cars were somewhat like modern military tanks. They were Citroën half-track vehicles, with continuous rubber treads around the rear wheels.

## FREE AT LAST

Gradually the idea of self-determination swept across the continent of Africa. Many nations embarked on struggles for independence after World War II (1939–1945). By the 1960s most of the Saharan lands had thrown off colonial rule and declared independence.

*Using special vehicles, the Haardt and Audouin-Dubreuil expedition of 1922–23 was the first crossing of the Sahara by automobile.*

It would seem that, by now, the Sahara would be thoroughly explored. Roads now connect many of the Sahara's cities, oasis towns, and mining sites. Where there are no roads, off-road vehicles cover many of the routes that ancient traders used to take. Yet, even today, vast areas of the Sahara have never been crossed by humans.

In spite of modernization, camel caravans still snake across great expanses of the Sahara to collect salt. With no trails to follow, the caravanners find their way as their ancestors did. They use the stars in the night sky to navigate the sea of sand. Though they know the desert well, they still respect its mysteries and its dangers.

◄ *Today, more regions of the Sahara are being explored than ever before.*

# FIVE

# Ways of Life in the Sahara

For thousands of years people have lived and worked in the Sahara region. In earlier times they enjoyed a lush landscape with rivers, lakes, and fertile farmland. That way of life ended when the Sahara became a desert. Yet, over the centuries, people still found ways to cross the Sahara, to work with its bleak conditions, and even to thrive there.

## LIFE IN A GREEN SAHARA

When the Sahara was rich with wildlife, people hunted large animals across the grasslands. Rock-art scenes at Algeria's Tassili n'Ajjer show people hunting buffaloes, elephants, and hippopotamuses. Their weapons were clubs, sticks, and axes. They also fished in the rivers and gathered wild grains beside the lakes and ponds.

Today it may be hard to imagine swimming in the Sahara. But swimming would have been an ordinary activity in earlier times. The Cave of Swimmers at Wadi Sura in southwestern Egypt shows many human figures swimming and diving.

◄ *The peoples of the Sahara have found the means to survive the harsh conditions of their environment.*

# Saharan Rock Art

The Sahara's rock artists used several different techniques. They carved images into rock by striking it with stone tools. For painted images they used colored mineral substances. Many paintings are reddish-brown, a color which is produced from iron oxide. For white paint, people used zinc oxide or kaolin, a type of clay. Charcoal or burnt bones produced the color black.

Some of the Sahara's most important rock art sites are Algeria's Tassili n'Ajjer, Libya's Tadrart Acacus, Niger's Ténéré and Nir, Chad's Tibesti Mountains, Mauritania's Dhar Tichitt, and various sites in southern Morocco. The first two have been declared World Heritage Sites by the United Nations Educational, Scientific and Cultural Organization (UNESCO). This designation guarantees them international funding and scientific support.

# DEALING WITH DESERTIFICATION

By about seven thousand years ago, Saharan people began settling in small villages, where they cultivated fields of millet. By this time they were herding animals they had tamed. Rock art from this era shows people tending cattle, sheep, and goats.

As desert conditions set in, the Sahara could no longer support large populations—neither human nor animal. By about 3000 B.C.E, Saharan farmers were abandoning their lands and moving out in mass migrations. Some went north, toward the Mediterranean coast. Others moved south into the forests and grasslands of central Africa. Thousands headed east into the Nile River Valley. Many historians believe this influx of people enabled the growth of the ancient Egyptian civilization along the Nile.

For the majority of Saharan people, leaving the arid wastelands seemed to offer their best chance for survival. Yet thousands decided to stay and try to build a new way of life. Across the Sahara, groups of people banded together in tribes. These various groups came to be called the Berbers.

Phoenician, Greek, Roman, and Byzantine people all crossed the Mediterranean and made settlements in North Africa. They all encountered native Berber peoples and kingdoms. The newcomers often entered into trade with the Berbers, offering wine and olive oil in exchange for salt and other goods.

## THE GARAMANTES

One group of Saharan people developed an ingenious way to thrive in the arid desert. Their culture is known as the Garamantes civilization. The Garamantes lived in the Fezzan region of central Libya from about 400 B.C.E to 600 C.E. Their capital city, Garama, was located at today's city of Germa.

The Garamantes had at least eight thriving towns and many outlying settlements. As many as ten thousand people lived there. They supplied gold, salt, glass, and precious gems to traders on the Mediterranean coast. As shown in their rock art, they transported goods in horse-drawn carts. Many Garamantes were farmers who raised abundant wheat, barley, and other crops. But how were they able to farm in the desert?

The Garamantes knew that pockets of water lay within the region's highlands. So they built *foggara*, or underground irrigation tunnels, out of stone. This network of tunnels transported water from the aquifer to their fields in the valley below. Almost 1,000 miles (1,600 km) of tunnels branched out across the land. All this came to an end, though. The Garamantes' aquifer was not an endless water source. After about a thousand years the water dried up, and the Garamantes civilization declined.

## ROMAN NORTH AFRICA

For more than a century, the Roman Empire tried to conquer Carthage. This city-state in today's Tunisia was too wealthy and

*The remains of a temple for the god ▶▶*
*Jupiter in Tunisia are a reminder of the*
*region's rule by the Roman Empire.*

powerful for Rome's taste. In 146 B.C.E, Rome finally destroyed Carthage. North Africa then became a province of the Roman Empire.

The Romans rebuilt Carthage, and under Roman rule, North Africa was richly productive. Farms in the region cultivated an estimated one million tons of grain every year. Other crops included olives, beans, and fruits such as figs and grapes. Eventually olive oil became the major export of Roman North Africa.

Ruling North Africa was not easy, though. Berber tribes of the Sahara waged constant attacks on Roman settlements. By this time the Berbers had formed the powerful kingdoms of Mauretania (present-day western Algeria and northern Morocco) and Numidia (northern and eastern Algeria). The Romans realized that there was a limit to how much territory they could control. As a defense against Berber raids, the Romans built a line of forts across the northern Sahara. Ruins of many of these forts still stand. By the 400s C.E., the declining Roman Empire lost its grip on North Africa.

## CAMELS AND ISLAM

Eventually the Sahara became so dry that horses could no longer make their way through the dusty, sandy soil. But by about the third century, camels had been introduced from the Arabian Peninsula.

These magnificent animals revolutionized trade in the Sahara. Berber merchants now traveled farther than ever before. With their camel caravans, they crossed the length and width of the Sahara.

*This painting depicts a mosque on a busy street in Algeria, illustrating the rule of Arab Muslims in North Africa.*

Oases were their way stations along the caravan routes. Both people and camels could rest and get fresh water there.

Another influence from Arabia had an even greater effect on the people of the Sahara. It was the religion of Islam. By 700 C.E. most of North Africa was under the control of Arab Muslims.

Thousands of Berber people converted to Islam. Under the Arabs, trans-Saharan trade expanded, too. One well-traveled route ran from Morocco to Timbuktu. Another stretched from Tunisia to Lake Chad. As traders traveled from one region to another, they spread Muslim culture and teachings throughout north and west Africa.

# West African Kingdoms

With the wealth from trans-Saharan trade, three great Muslim kingdoms arose on the southwestern fringes of the Sahara. The Ghana Empire flourished from about 750 to 1076 in southern Mauritania and Mali. The Mali Empire (c. 1235–1468) stretched from its capital at Timbuktu westward to the Atlantic Ocean. The empire reached its height under its greatest emperor, Mansa Musa. The Songhai Empire, from its capital city of Gao (Mali), gradually took over the Mali Empire's territory. Expanding as far as present-day Nigeria, it remained in power until the late 1500s.

## THE TRANS-SAHARAN TRADE

Trade centers such as Timbuktu became lively, multicultural cities. Arabs, Berbers, and peoples from south of the Sahara all met in their bustling marketplaces. For scholars and students, books were the most desirable trade items, and the book trade was a highly profitable business. Some traders brought goods up the Niger River by boat. Thus trade goods from deep in central Africa could reach the Mediterranean coast. From there they were shipped on to Europe and the Middle East.

On southbound caravan routes, trade goods included guns and woven cloth. On northbound routes, gold and salt were among the most prized African goods. Other treasures were copper, spices, ivory, ostrich feathers, and exotic animals. However, one of the most valuable trade items was slaves.

Slavery was common in central Africa. One tribe acquired slaves through raids or warfare with another tribe. In the days of trans-Saharan trade, millions of people were sold as slaves to merchant caravans. The slaves were marched northward across the Sahara with shackles around their necks. As many as half of them died along the way. Those who survived were sold to serve in households in North Africa and the Middle East.

The trans-Saharan trade began to decline in the 1500s. Portugal had developed a formidable fleet of merchant ships, and Portuguese navigators regularly sailed to West African ports. Gradually Europe

*A slave caravan stops to rest on its trans-Saharan route.*

became the major consumer of African goods. It was far easier and less expensive to transport those goods to Europe by ship than by overland caravan routes. Although some caravans still trekked across the searing desert sands, the era of trans-Saharan trade was over.

## PEOPLE OF THE SAHARA TODAY

Today only about 2.5 million people live throughout the entire Sahara region. About three-fourths of those people live in oasis areas. Using irrigation, they raise a variety of fruits, vegetables, and grains. People who live in the Sahara's dry regions are nomads. They live by herding camel, cattle, sheep, or goats. From time to time they visit the oases to trade and to get water and other supplies.

Many Saharan peoples are Berbers or mixtures of Berber and Arab ethnic groups. The major peoples of the Sahara today are the Moors, the Tuareg, and the Toubou (also spelled Tubu, Tibbu, Tebu, or Tebou). Minority ethnic groups, many of whom have mixed with Berbers and Arabs, include the Hausa, Djerma, Fulani, Bambara, Malinke, Soninke, and Sara.

## THE MOORS

The name *Moors* is sometimes used for the Muslims who occupied Spain, Portugal, and North Africa in the Middle Ages. Throughout history the name has been used to designate a variety of North African peoples. Ancient Romans, for example, used the term *Mauri* for peoples who lived in the Roman province of Mauretania. That term, in turn, may have come from the ancient Berber kingdom of the Maure tribe. Most properly, though, Moors are a North African ethnic group who speak the Hassaniya dialect of Arabic.

Today's Moors live in Mauritania and Western Sahara, as well as Morocco, Mali, and Niger. Ethnically they may be a mixture of Berber, Arab, and black African people. Traditionally most Moors lead nomadic or seminomadic lives. They herd camels and goats and dig deep into the desert sands to make wells.

In Mauritania Moors make up more than half the population. They are divided into the White Moors (Bidan) and the Black Moors (Haratin). White Moors make up the upper class, while Black Moors belong to the slave class. Slavery has been practiced in Mauritania for eight hundred years. Although it has been abolished, the practice continues. Freed slaves are now pushing for stricter antislavery laws. Unfortunately, though, many slaves believe that they belong in slavery or that their situation is hopeless.

## THE TOUBOU

The traditional homeland of the Toubou is the Tibesti Mountain region of northern Chad. The Toubou were trading with the ancient city of Carthage as early as 500 B.C.E. Today many Toubou still live in the Tibesti region. They are often called the Teda Toubou. Another group live in southern Chad. They are called the Daza Toubou, although many Daza also live in the north. Other Toubou live in Libya, Niger, and Sudan.

Traditionally the Toubou are nomadic herders. Today some Toubou live by raising herds of camels, sheep, goats, cattle, or horses. Others are seminomadic, returning to oasis villages during rainy seasons. In the villages, some Toubou live a settled life, raising date palms, grains, and other crops. Their homes are mud or stone huts with roofs of thatched palm leaves.

The Toubou are organized into clans, and members are very loyal to their fellow clansmen. They help each other in times of need and are forbidden to steal from one another. Certain clans have exclusive rights to specific water springs, palm groves, and grazing lands. Among the Teda Toubou, the *derde* is the spiritual and political leader. The Toubou were major fighters in Chad's civil war (1965–1979). Rivalry between ethnic groups played a major part in the conflict.

# THE TUAREG

The Tuareg are one of the Berber ethnic groups of north and west Africa. Most Tuareg live in Niger, Mali, Algeria, Libya, and Burkina Faso. They have been called the "blue men of the desert." The name refers to the indigo-blue turbans and face coverings that Tuareg men wear. The blue dye from the cloth can give their skin a bluish tint.

The Tuareg call themselves *Kel Tamasheq*, meaning "speakers of the Tamasheq language." They write in an ancient script called Tifinagh. Another name the Tuareg use is *Imashagen*, meaning "noble and free." They value their independence and their centuries-old freedom to roam across the vast Sahara. At times they have fought fiercely to maintain that freedom.

*The Tuareg are recognized by the blue turbans that they wear.*

When the French colonized west Africa they challenged the Tuaregs' freedom. The French drew boundary lines across Tuareg territory. They took over Tuareg grazing lands, interrupted their trade, and enlisted them as soldiers and laborers. In the twentieth century the Tuareg way of life broke down even more. Thousands of Tuareg were moved to refugee camps and unfamiliar towns. The Tuareg Rebellion (1990–1996) resulted in some benefits. However, it did not lead to an independent Tuareg state, as many had hoped.

## TRADITIONAL TUAREG LIFE

Today, as in the past, Tuareg people live mainly in the western part of the Sahara—predominantly in Algeria, Niger, and Mali. Although the desert is their domain, they often camp in the Sahara's mountains, where they find water and cool air. Tamanrasset, in Algeria's Ahaggar Mountains, is a major center for Algeria's Tuareg people. Agadez, at the base of Niger's Aïr Mountains, is the Tuareg capital of that region.

Many of the Sahara's Tuareg raise camels, moving to new pasture-lands from time to time. Their traditional dwelling is a tent made of hides dyed red. Some Tuareg have settled into a farming life. Others are blacksmiths who make intricate silver jewelry.

Tuareg salt traders still lead their camel caravans for hundreds of miles across the desert. In Niger they follow their traditional route from Agadez to Bilma to collect salt. They load their camels with huge, cone-shaped blocks of salt, as well as goatskins filled with dates. Some caravans return to Agadez, while others trek south to Nigeria.

There they trade the salt for millet, cloth, household utensils, and other goods.

In Mali, Tuareg caravans travel from Timbuktu to the remote and desolate salt mines of Taoudenni. Once their camels are laden with slabs of salt, they begin their long journey back to Timbuktu. Along the way they pass skeletons of long-dead camels bleached white in the sun. They are grim reminders of the harshness of desert life.

## OASIS SETTLEMENTS

About three-fourths of the Sahara's people live in oasis settlements. A spring or well is the hub of an oasis. One oasis might be as small as a well with a few palm trees growing around it. Most oases have fewer than two thousand residents.

There are only about ninety large oases in the Sahara. Some are busy communities with paved streets and many buildings. Others have sandy streets lined by sand-colored homes and shops. Shady palm groves and leafy gardens thrive against the desert backdrop.

People in oases grow dates, figs, peaches, citrus fruits, barley, wheat, and vegetables. Irrigation canals branch out from the water source to the fields. Each farm family might be assigned certain days when it can use the water. In some

*Fewer than one hundred large oases can be found in the Sahara. El-Oued is an oasis town in Algeria.*

oases, people plant date palms as fences to keep drifting sand from covering their homes.

Not all oasis villages win this battle against the sands. The village of Araouane, Mali, is slowly getting buried. People constantly sweep and dig the sand from their doorways to save their homes. Still the sands advance, and people must rebuild their houses above sand level every few years. Some oasis villagers lose the battle, though. They give up and move somewhere else. In time there is no trace left of their old town.

## ROADS AND TRACKS

People in the Sahara still use camels to get around. However, paved roads now connect many oasis towns and follow some of the old caravan routes. Paved roads also lead to some mining centers.

Construction began on the north–south Trans-Sahara Highway in 1971. It was intended to run from the Algerian coast all the way to Nigeria. However, the project was abandoned before it was finished. Another Trans-Sahara Highway is being built near the Atlantic coast from Morocco through Western Sahara and Mauritania to Senegal. Then it will head east, eventually reaching Nigeria. All these highways face one big problem. Sand keeps blowing across them and covering them up.

Vehicles can also follow the *pistes*. These are unpaved routes where desert traffic has worn tracks in the dust and sand. This can be dangerous, though. When desert winds blow sand over the tracks, vehicles can get stuck in the sand or lost.

# RACING ACROSS THE SAHARA

As if to defy the dangers of desert travel, people hold road races in the Sahara. The Paris-Dakar Rally used to run from Paris, France, to Dakar, Senegal. That included a ferry ride across the Mediterranean Sea. Now called the Dakar Rally, its starting point varies, though it still ends in Dakar. Off-road vehicles, motorcycles, and trucks take part, tearing across mud, sand dunes, and rocks.

For the ultimate endurance test, runners race across the Sahara. The Marathon des Sables (Marathon of the Sands) is the toughest footrace on Earth. This six-day event covers about 150 miles (240 kilometers) of desert in southern Morocco. In temperatures of 120°F (49°C) or more, the runners dash across treacherous dunes and rocks.

Another footrace, the Sahara Marathon, takes place near Tindouf, Algeria. It is held in support of the Saharawi people of Western Sahara who are refugees from their war-torn homeland. Yet another race covers 150 miles (240 km) of Egypt's Western Desert.

Sahara marathoners trudge through sandstorms, hobble on blistered feet, and **hallucinate** from lack of sleep. They might spot vultures circling overhead. One race even charges a fee in advance for returning a body to its home country! Why do people put themselves through such an ordeal? No one really explains it well. One runner in the Marathon des Sables said, "Because this is the desert." Another replied, "Because I am mad"—meaning crazy.

# SIX

# Preserving a Fragile Environment

The Sahara has existed as a desert for thousands of years. During that time it has changed very little. Winds have shifted the sands. Waters have given life to scattered oases. And relentless heat has discouraged all but the hardiest creatures.

Humans, as well as animals, have learned to deal with the Sahara's stark realities. Many people have crossed the desert. Others have learned to survive on its fringes or around its precious oases. Yet all have held a profound respect for the natural forces at work in the Sahara.

Only in the twentieth century did people begin to make large-scale alterations in the desert to meet human needs. These changes have had profound effects on the desert **ecosystem**.

Natural forces are altering the Sahara, too. Over time, global climate changes transformed the Sahara from an arid wasteland to a lush grassland and back again. Are natural climate changes at work in the Sahara again? Are humans speeding up the process, or slowing

◄ *The Sahara is a living desert, where today, its preservation is crucial for the peoples and wildlife that call it home.*

it down? We can examine these questions, although scientists will continue to debate them for years to come.

## MORE PEOPLE, GREATER NEEDS

Africa's population is growing quickly. According to the United Nations Population Fund, the average **fertility rate** in Africa in 2007 was almost five births per woman. In spite of high death rates as well, Africa is still the fastest-growing region in the world. Between 1960 and 2000 Africa's population almost tripled. (During that same time, North America's population rose 50 percent, and Europe's increased only 20 percent.)

*Population growth will have an adverse effect on the Sahara's limited underground water supply.*

How does population growth affect the Sahara? It has many consequences. Even with irrigation, cropland in the Sahara is scarce. With more mouths to feed, people risk depleting the nutrients in the soil.

Water resources in the Sahara are scarce, too. The growing population needs more and more water to survive. Pumping water from underground sources seems a good solution. Yet the demand for water can outstrip the supply. The Sahara's aquifers can recharge, or refill with water, but this can take hundreds or even thousands of years.

## DEFORESTATION

**Deforestation** might not seem to be a problem for the vast, virtually treeless Sahara. However, it is a major environmental problem in the Sahel, along the Sahara's southern edge. As trees are stripped from the Sahel, the moisture held in their leaves and roots is lost as well. Less soil is held in place, too, leading to the erosion of fertile soils. As a result the arid desert's border creeps farther south.

*Malians severely strain the region's forest resources by using more than 5 million tons of wood per year.*

Deforestation is a serious issue in countries where the Sahara meets the Sahel. Mali is just one example. Most of this country lies within the Sahara. However, the Niger River runs through southern Mali. Savannah woodlands flourish in this region, and most of Mali's farming and other economic activities take place here.

According to Mali's ministry of the environment, Malians use about 6 million tons (5.4 million metric tons) of wood every year. Some is used as household or industrial fuel, and some is used as timber for construction and other industries. This removes about 1,540 square miles (4,000 sq. km) of tree growth a year. With such a high rate of deforestation, the Sahara is bound to reach even deeper into the country.

## DROUGHTS: POOR LAND MANAGEMENT?

Severe droughts struck the Sahara and the Sahel in the 1970s and 1980s. The lack of rain led to widespread famine. Cracks appeared in the parched ground, and vital food crops shriveled in the sun. Hundreds of thousands of people died of starvation. Millions of camels, sheep, and goats died off, too. This forced many Tuareg and other nomadic herders to abandon their traditional lifestyles. They crowded into cities already strained with starving people.

Droughts have devastating effects on the Sahara's environment and human populations. But what causes these droughts? There are several theories. Some scientists say they are caused by too much farming and grazing in the Sahel.

According to this theory, overfarming depletes the soil, making it unable to support plant life. Overgrazing has the same effect, as large herds of camels, cattle, and other livestock eat away the ground cover. The ground, stripped of plants, then reflects more sunlight. The sun's rays radiate up into the atmosphere and heat it, creating layers of hot, dry air above the ground. This air prevents moist rain clouds from forming in the atmosphere.

## CLIMATE CYCLES AND GLOBAL WARMING

Some scientists say droughts in the Sahara region are the result of natural climate cycles. They say it is not unusual for years of drought to be followed by years of plentiful rain. Other scientists say the droughts are caused by changes in the temperatures of the world's oceans. Still others say Africa's droughts are due to global warming—a climate change that affects the whole planet.

The global warming theory gained momentum in the early twenty-first century. That is partly due to findings of the Intergovernmental Panel on Climate Change. This group is made up of leading scientists from around the world. After years of studies they released a report in 2007. The Earth's climate is definitely growing warmer, they reported.

According to the panel, global warming has a severe effect on regions that are already semiarid, such as the Sahel. Between 1900 and 2005 the Sahel has become increasingly drier. This trend had its worst effects in the droughts of the 1970s and 1980s.

Some scientists predict 30 percent less rainfall in the Sahel in the twenty-first century. If these predictions are accurate, droughts will continue to plague the region, and the Sahara will continue to expand southward over time.

# The Greenhouse Effect

Most experts agree that human activities are causing global warming. Factories and vehicles release carbon dioxide, methane, and other gases into the atmosphere. These "greenhouse gases" let sunlight in but keep heat from escaping, much like a greenhouse does. This condition is called the greenhouse effect. Climatologists say this could cause the Earth's average temperature to rise between 3° and 8° F (16° and 13° C) during the twenty-first century. Africa produces the world's lowest levels of greenhouse gases. However, it suffers some of the worst effects of global warming.

## URBANIZATION AND AQUIFERS

**Urbanization** is one effect of population growth in the Sahara. As the population grows, fewer people can make a living from the desert's meager resources. As a result, more and more people migrate from rural areas to the cities. The growing cities need more and more water for drinking, cooking, bathing, and industrial activities. Where does this water come from? As you might expect, it comes from the Sahara's underground water sources.

Libya provides a good example. Most of its population lives in the coastal cities, and those cities are growing steadily. However, aquifers near the coast are contaminated with salty seawater, and residents need fresh drinking water. Libya addressed this problem

*Libyans celebrate in the waters of one of the dams built to store water in the Great Manmade River project.*

with its Great Manmade River (GMR) project. This is the largest water-supply project in the world. It carries water by pipeline from aquifers deep in the desert to the coastal cities.

Next Libya plans to use irrigation from the aquifers to add hundreds of thousands of acres of new farmland. In places where nothing would grow before, farmers will be able to raise wheat, oats, corn, and barley. These are crops that Libya has had to import in the past. Still, no one knows how long the water supply will last. If the aquifers run dry, the effects on Libya's economy would be devastating.

## DISAPPEARING SPECIES

Many animals of the Sahara are disappearing. As farming regions expand, overgrazing reduces the animals' food supply. As urban centers grow, human populations strain the animals' water supplies. However, hunting takes the greatest toll on the Sahara's animal life.

Animals are most at risk in oasis areas and along the fringes of the desert, where there is more rainfall. Animals are drawn to these places to find water. Unfortunately, humans live there for the same reason, and they hunt animals such as oryxes and addaxes for their meat.

Hunting for sport has done even more harm. Thanks to overhunting, the addax is almost extinct, and several antelope species are endangered. Hunters have completely wiped out the scimitar-horned oryx. Great herds of this horselike antelope once ranged along the Sahara's northern and southern edges. But the Sahara's last remaining oryxes disappeared in the 1990s. Most Saharan nations have also outlawed hunting. These laws are often hard to enforce, though.

The loss of one animal species has an impact on other species as well. Gazelles, for example, are a major food source for cheetahs. As gazelles become more scarce, cheetahs have a harder time surviving. Cheetahs themselves are hunted, too.

## WORKING TOGETHER ON SOLUTIONS

Many international organizations are working on the Sahara's environmental and conservation issues. In the wildlife arena, one is the Sahara Conservation Fund (SCF). It conducts programs such as breeding Saharan ostriches to release into the wild. The SCF is also working with the government of Tunisia to reintroduce addaxes and oryxes into the wild.

# Animals at Risk

The World Conservation Union, or International Union for the Conservation of Nature and Natural Resources (IUCN), gives the following classifications to these Sahara animals:

| | |
|---|---|
| Addax | Critically endangered |
| Barbary sheep | Vulnerable |
| Cheetah | Vulnerable |
| Dama gazelle | Critically endangered |
| Dorcas gazelle | Vulnerable |
| Sand cat | Near threatened |
| Scimitar-horned oryx | Extinct in the wild |
| Striped hyena | Near threatened |

The Convention on the Conservation of Migratory Species of Wild Animals (CMS) is another international animal-protection organization. It is an agency of the United Nations (UN). Member nations—including Saharan countries—aim to protect animals that naturally migrate across national borders.

Keeping the desert from advancing is an international concern. It is the focus of the United Nations Convention to Combat

Desertification (UNCCD). More than 170 nations have signed this agreement, including all the Saharan nations. It emphasizes action at the community level to promote sustainable development in semiarid regions so deserts will not spread. About two-thirds of the Saharan countries have drawn up national action programs.

Protecting the Sahara's aquifers is also a vital issue. Some countries are more aggressive than others in tapping into the aquifers. Experts predict that the competition for water could lead to "water wars." To address this problem the UN organized a project called Internationally Shared Aquifer Resource Management (ISARM). It is working out guidelines for managing Saharan aquifers.

Preserving the Sahara and its resources is not just an African issue. It is a worldwide concern. Many of us may never get closer to the Sahara than seeing zoo animals or watching a TV show or movie. But the vast Sahara—with its landscape, wildlife, culture, and legends—is a part of our shared awareness. We can imagine the Sahara in all its splendor, and we can benefit from exploring its mysteries.

The more scientists learn about the Earth, the more we discover how interconnected we are. The same atmosphere surrounds us all. The exhaust from our vehicles can make the Sahara warmer, and the Sahara's dust may end up in our own backyards! From this point of view, the Sahara seems not so far away after all.

*For thousands of years the great Sahara has been a place of wonder and mystery for all who have walked its sands.*

# Glossary

**biodiversity**  the presence of a variety of different animal and plant species

**contiguous**  connected; touching one another

**deforestation**  the removal of trees and other forest vegetation

**desertification**  the process of becoming a desert

**ecosystem**  a community of organisms that work together within an environment

**fertility rate**  the rate of births within a population group

**hallucinate**  to see visions of things that do not exist

**massifs**  groups of connected mountains

**sustainable development**  development of land and other natural resources in a way that does not damage or use up those resources

**urbanization**  the growth of cities as people leave rural areas

# Fast Facts

**Name:** Sahara (Arabic: *as-sahra*, meaning "desert")

**Location:** North Africa, covering parts of Morocco, Western Sahara, Mauritania, Algeria, Tunisia, Mali, Niger, Libya, Chad, Egypt, and Sudan

**Area:** About 3.5 million square miles (9 million sq. km)

**Greatest dimensions:** North to south: more than 1,200 miles (1,930 km); east to west: more than 3,500 miles (5,630 km)

**Borders:** Atlas Mountains and Mediterranean Sea to the north; Sahel region on the south; Atlantic Ocean on the west; Red Sea on the east

**Highest elevation:** Emi (Mount) Koussi, in the Tibesti Mountains of Chad at 11,204 feet (3,415 m)

**Lowest elevation:** Qattara Depression in Egypt at 436 feet (133 m) below sea level)

**Average temperatures:** Summer: 90°–110 °F (32°–43 °C); Winter: 50° to 60 °F (10° to 16 °C)

**Average precipitation:** 3 inches (76 mm) a year

**Population:** About 2.5 million (late 1990s est.)

**Major ethnic groups:** Tuareg, Toubou, Moor, Berber, Arab

**Languages spoken:** Arabic, French, Tamasheq, various Berber dialects

**Famous explorers:** Ibn Battuta, Mungo Park, Alexander Gordon Laing, Réné Caillié, Heinrich Barth

**Famous sites:** Djenné Mosque (Mali) Germa archaeological site (Libya)

*Djenné Mosque*

Roman amphitheater at El Jem (Tunisia)
Roman ruins at Leptis Magna and Ghadames (Libya)
Tadrart Acacus rock art (Libya)
Tassili n'Ajjer rock art (Algeria)
Timbuktu (Mali)

*Dama gazelle*

**Animals:** Camels, gazelles, antelopes, Barbary sheep, foxes, sand cats, hyenas, jackals, snakes, lizards, jerboas and other rodents

**Plants:** Acacia trees, palm trees, various hardy shrubs and grasses

**Major rivers:** Nile River, Niger River

**Largest lake:** Lake Chad

**Mountain ranges:** Tibesti Massif (Chad), Ahaggar Mountains (Algeria), Aïr Massif (Niger), Tassili n'Ajjer (Algeria)

**Major ergs (dune regions):** Grand Erg Oriental (Algeria, Tunisia), Grand Erg Occidental (Algeria), Great Sand Sea (Egypt), Idehan Murzuq (Libya), Great Bilma Erg (Niger), Erg Chech (Algeria)

**Economic resources:** Water, salt, petroleum and natural gas, copper, iron, phosphates, uranium, manganese, tin, nickel, chromium, zinc, lead, cobalt, silver, gold

**Greatest threats:** Desertification, water depletion, oversettlement, deforestation, animal endangerment

# Find Out More

## BOOKS

Barber, Nicola. *Living in the Sahara.* Chicago: Raintree, 2008.

Goss, Linda C. *Exploring Mali: A Young Person's Guide to Ancient Civilization.* Norfolk, VA: Maya Publications, 2006.

Haldane, Elizabeth. *Desert: Around the Clock with the Animals of the Desert.* New York: DK Children, 2006.

Lappi, Megan. *The Sahara Desert.* New York: Weigl Publishers, 2006.

Mitchell, Peter, ed. *Peoples and Cultures of North Africa.* New York: Facts on File, 2006.

Reynolds, Jan. *Sahara: Vanishing Cultures.* New York: Lee & Low Books, 2006.

## WEB SITES

**Africa—Explore the Regions: Sahara**
www.pbs.org/wnet/africa/explore/sahara/sahara_overview_lo.html
An easy-to-read look at the Sahara's landforms, people, animals, and plants.

**Deserts and Desertification**
www.visumtourism.ch/deserts2006/
For information on the growth of deserts, climate factors, and nomadic peoples.

**Oxfam's Cool Planet: The Sahara Desert**
www.oxfam.org.uk/coolplanet/ontheline/explore/nature/deserts/sahara.htm
For discussions of the Sahara's landscapes, plants and animals, and conservation issues.

**The 153 Club**
www.the153club.org/
For Sahara travelers, a tour through the desert's ancient and modern explorations, ancient cultures, forts, and rock art.

# Index

Page numbers in **boldface** are illustrations and charts.

Roman temple, **63**

## ABOUT THE AUTHOR

Ann Heinrichs loves traveling to faraway places, and deserts are her favorite terrain. She has camped among nomads of the Sahara, cheered their camel races, and enjoyed their traditional songs.

In Niger, she visited the ancient city of Agadez, climbed the foothills of the Aïr Mountains, explored the stark Ténéré Desert, and slept on the desert floor. Under magnificent starry skies, she huddled around Tuareg campfires as they told legends and served aromatic tea. Writing this book brought back many memories of breathtaking landscapes and warm, friendly people.

Heinrichs grew up roaming the woods behind her home in Fort Smith, Arkansas. Now she lives in Chicago, Illinois. She is the author of more than two hundred books for children and young adults on U.S. and world history and culture.